the ocean is quiet
and wide as the sky.
the waves whisper
as they kiss the shore
and tell secrets
to the pebbles and sand.

I stand on a bridge
suspended between
the lifetime before
and the lifetime to come;
and wish on an invisible star
that I may carry my learning with me.

~ **Candice James**

Also by Candice James

10 PAK - 2
10 PAK - 1
A Potpourri of Paintings
The Still Small Voice of Soul
Spiritual Whispers
Atmospheres
Blue Silence
Call of the Crow
Imagination's Reverie
Short Shots 2
The Depth of the Dance
Behind the One-Way Mirror
The Path of Loneliness
Rithimus Aeternam
The Water Poems
Short Shots
City of Dreams
Merging Dimensions
The 13th Cusp
Colors of India
Purple Haze
A Silence of Echoes
Shorelines
Ekphrasticism
Midnight Embers
Bridges and Clouds
Inner Heart, a Journey
A Split in the Water

10 PAK – 3

THE LONG POEMS

by
Candice James

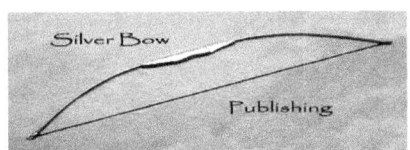

Box 5 – 720 – 6th Street,
New Westminster, BC
V3C 3C5   CANADA

Title: 10 PAK -3 The Long Poems
Author: Candice James
Copyright © 2025 Silver Bow Publishing
Cover Painting: "Everest"
　　　　　　　　painting by Candice James
Layout/Design: Candice James
ISBN: 9781774033609 (print)
ISBN: 9781774033616 (ebk)j

All rights reserved including the right to reproduce or translate this book or any portions thereof, in any form except for the use of short passages for review purposes, no part of this book may be reproduced, in part or in whole, or transmitted in any form or by any means, electronically or mechanically, including photocopying, recording, or any information or storage retrieval system without prior permission in writing from the publisher or a license from the Canadian Copyright Collective Agency (Access Copyright)
© Silver Bow Publishing 2025

Library and Archives Canada Cataloguing in Publication

FOREWORD

The poems in this book are long poems set out in such a way as to allow the reader to rest on each page to fully digest the meaning and let their imagination run free to see the visuals and images the words are painting.

This layout gives the reader the best of experiences as they go through the poems and pages.

10 PAK -3 The Long Poems – *Candice James*

CONTENTS

The "I Am" / 9

Never-Ending Moment in Eternity / 37

I Am Alive / 59

Time / 79

Rain / 87

Stone Night / 95

Visions and Impressions of the 7th Kind / 107

Leaving and Staying / 119

Frayed Edges / 131

I Rise / 151

Author Profile / 168

10 PAK -3 The Long Poems – *Candice James*

The "I Am"

PAK -3 The Long Poems – *Candice James*

I am the I Am

out-picturing myself
to become
the reality I am

I am

the ever-present moving mist
visible, invisible, hot, cold
and "the all"
in between
the in-between

I put paint to paper
and pen to canvas
exchanging realms and mediums;
comfort and discomforts
holding hands
as they survey
their new surroundings

Human interactions and intercourse
Are ascribed to inanimate objects
something like emotions
to flesh and bone

And we rock and we roll
in the palm of life
listening and dancing
to the music of the stars
on a spring-a-lator dance floor
suspended in the ether

Burning the candlewax
down to the wick
lighting up the ebony edge
of a crisp midnight
in the relentless push and pull
of lust and love

The abstraction of time
in a rotating universe
is a synaptic flash
in the mind of the eternal

Musical time signatures
echo in my memories
sewing them to fading footprints
and ebbing voices

Sanity and stupor
walk hand in hand
through my waking dreams
in a fragile wonderland
of pulsating colors

Kicking up dust
as I walk between graveyards,
I cement a posse past
to the fleeing future
in the overgrown cemetery
of the unsuspecting present
where my presence is
regarded and disregarded
in the higher university
of reverie and contempt

Separately encompassed
in a simulcast sound wave
I float through the ether
for five to seven eternities
then come to coveted rest
on the sixth step of sentience

In this realm of the visibly invisible
I am a vapid ghost
viewing and reviewing all things
inside-out, outside in,
topsy turvy and bottom to top
through the myriad of eyes
that are watching me
and tunneling deeply
into my inner soul

I looked inside tomorrow
and saw music
I walked through yesterday
and heard moonbeams
I embraced the rhythm
of dissolving moments
and danced into
a disappearing dream

The breeze called my name
in dampened whispers
and the trees rustled
in tones soft and low

Tones only I could hear,
only I could understand

And I swear I heard one tree
shed a heavy tear
as I was drawn to its trunk
of harbored wounds,
landlocked in desperation's
tight yet tender embrace

And I swear when I looked,
that tree had a face
and sap dribbled and ran
from its age-worn knot-holes,
slow like a centipede's ship
of sorrows and tepid tears
adrift on a tangled ocean

Alms for oblivion
and penance for paupers
in this strange world
of periods and commas,
dangling modifiers
and fragmented sentences
screaming for attention
and alterations
in this pre-school academy
of errors and omissions

Climbing over
a charcoal horizon
a colorful bird of lost causes
slowly surfaces in a haze

A rainforest phoenix
lost in a dry-drunk desert
peppered with rundown
and abandoned skid row bars,
empty eyes, broken bottles,
drunken butterflies
and derelict dragonflies

And in this chaotic senseless scene
I am bound in rusty cuffs,
bearing false witness
and dying of a never-ending thirst
inside a burnt and bleeding dune
of desecrated crystal snow

I lay spent and motionless
on a slice of static water
and my eyes keep icing over
in this solid evanescent sea

Everything is bright light
and spinning neon white
shining sparkles on my linen paper
as I write my temporary epitaph
indelibly and indefinitely
with invisible ink,
thinned with tears
and dropped from the wearied
and lackluster eyes of time
I peer through with trepidation

I rise up from this damp bed
of ashes and burnt embers,
I become a thin wisp of smoke

I am above and below
I am here and beyond
I am the invisible visible
I am the square root
and the circular information

I am the
informational
reciprocal

I am life and death
without end

I am one with the soils of the sky
and bred into and imbedded
in the diamonds of the sea

I am a rare, emblazoned jewel
amongst semi-precious stones.
I shine precious in the rarefied eyes
of Orion's only child

I am the high priestess
of the seven moving mists

I am the fish, the animal, the bird
I am the woman, the man, the other
I am the tumultuous oceans
and the serene skies

I am the all in the nothing at all.

I am the emptiness
in the fullness therein

I am the vessel
     of
   the "I am"

I am the residue of the nothing
that flourishes into something

I have always been
and will always be:

> In flesh
> In spirit
> In water
> In sky

Exchanging realms
and mediums...

I am
"the I am" ...

I am

10 PAK -3 The Long Poems – *Candice James*

Never-Ending Moment in Eternity

10 PAK -3 The Long Poems – *Candice James*

I am present
now,
in the past
and in the future

I am familiar with
the difference
in tense and sound
of the silence and the echoes

In my realm
of thinking and living
time is never of the essence

It is simply a static passing
of images, voices and ghosts

In my world, sunlight drifts
with the wind and rain
and holds hands
with the mist and fog

I peer through the half-lidded eyes
of a pulsating intelligence
that has fallen away from reality
and now walks as a ghost
through the transient dreams
of a million new-born stars

Some destined to sparkle brightly
Some destined to shoot across my sky
and some destined to burn out
in a blurred molecular implosion

I am privy to what is
and what was,
what could have been
and what is now

And what is NOW
is but a short-lived second
and most seconds pass
unceremoniously
into the hungry portal of "then"

So "now"
equates with "is"
and "then"
equates with "was"
and "will be" and "can be"
    "may be."

'NOW"
is a static stationary point.

"THEN"
is a fluxuating non-fixed point.

I am both

Inhabiting a state of flesh and bone
I am a static stationary point
somehow moving but not moving
through all my moments of "now",
becoming all my "thens"
and possibilities
to shape and reshape my "nows"
as I drift through non-existent time

"TIME" is not and we are not
in this holographic non-reality,
this dream
God is dreaming

But, God is benevolent
and all-forgiving
so we are given free will
and we either sink or swim
in this vast sea of nothingness
we believe to be everything

And now I must speak of soul.

    The spirit
which resides in us all

I look at the blank paper on my desk.
I look at my hand writing words
and I look at the pen it wills
so effortlessly to move across the page

I seem to be solid, more than a ghost,
but I know I am not flesh and bone

I know my body is just a vehicle,
a mirage of atoms, dust and air

I am almost unnoticeable
a temporary ghost in a hologram
moving around, navigating the ether

We are the rain
created by falling teardrops;
each one landing, pooling, then dissolving
in the heat of God's breath

And this dissolving, this death,
is what we are born for
again and again

We are continuously short-lived
parading through the ages
in a series of long successions

We are the roses growing in concrete,
We are the fish living in high-rises.
We are the birds walking the streets.
We are elephants writing in Sanskrit
We are the bodies invading the ghosts
We are the atoms invading the vacuum
We are life forever chasing death

And we live and construct and demolish
in our sojourns between breath and death
reaping what we have sown,
spending minutes in paradise
and hours in horror.

I awoke this morning
and became the air

I sat on a park bench at mid-day,
feet on the ground, I became the soil

I wandered a sandy beach in early evening
wading a shoreline and became the water

I looked up at a sparkling sky at midnight
I freed my mind and became the stars

Then I passed back
into my flesh and bone
and closed my eyes to sleep softly
and enter back into the dream I am

I rise and I fall
I crumble and resurrect
I am destroyed and rebuilt

I endure

I am the soil and the sky
I am the moon and the stars
I am the essence of air
I am the wet of water
held in the sighs and tears
of this, the majesty and magic
of a never-ending moment in eternity

10 PAK -3 The Long Poems – *Candice James*

I'm Alive

10 PAK -3 The Long Poems – *Candice James*

I stand on the glossy surface
of a smooth early morning ocean
I touch the sky in a dissolving embrace

A scent of salt and roses drifts in
on the blossoming breeze

I feel the sun warming my cheeks
I feel the rain wetting my face

    I am alive

I am a rock, heavy with tears
crumbling beneath a fading sun

Dusk enters on soft satin slippers
A glimmering evening star appears
Then everything dissolves into a speck

The speck vibrates and expands
A jewelled ladder materializes.
suspended in a golden aura of light

I step onto the first rung of the ladder
I take a deep breath and begin climbing

All around me is a glowing kaleidoscope
of oscillating rainbows and mirrors

I am a rock disintegrating
into a spirit of shimmering bright
expunging the dark of night

I rise as a Lark at glorious sunrise
to fly like an eagle into paradise

I travel millions of miles to find my rest

Weary...
I fell into a deep sleep of dreams
where I stood inside myself once again

I witnessed air turning to water
and water changing into stone
then evaporating into air
and on and on the cycle continued

I saw myself in a capsule of air,
a bubble floating aimlessly,
in a semi-haze of iridescent fog.

A large zipper suddenly appeared
and opened to a bevy of light

    Stars sparkled,
      voices sang
and angels hovered in throngs

I was lifted and slung high
into the realm of spitirual life
on the other side of reality
where everything unknown is known
and everything blocked and hidden
is exposed, revealed and familiar

I stood at attention,
alert, yet fully relaxed

I moved my lips to speak
but I could not form words

It did not matter

My thoughts spoke louder
    than speech
and were understood
    absolutely

A pale nondescript moth
approached and alit silently
onto my left shoulder

Slowly its wings unravelled
in a splendiferous and majestic
vibrating rainbow of metallic colors

It became a creature
more beautiful
than a butterfly
or a dragonfly

It held me entranced
with its sharp eyes

Somehow, it miniaturized me
so I could ride safely on its wings
and we flew far and away
to a world of fantastical visions

There were pale blue brick roads
leading into pastel pink forests

There was beautiful music all around
and beautiful creatures relaxing
in the depth of their own smiles

On the other side of the blue road,
there was a beach of cotton sand
and an ocean of pistachio tea

A world of dreams flew overhead;
beautiful kites of wishes and promises
dotted the magnificent scene

I was handed the guide string of a kite
and told to pull it down from the sky

When I held it in my hand it pulsated
and grew into a full-figured man

A man that wasn't a man at all.
but an entity that was a shapeshifter

Suddenly it was my childhood dog
then my mother smoking a cigarette
then my father drinking a glass of rye
my grandmother baking cookies
my grandfather sawing a driftwood log
on a sawhorse and me sitting on the log

In split second
I wasn't watching me anymore
I was actually sitting on the log
I was young again... 7 years old

Then, out of the blue, a bolt —
and a luminous being
drifted at my side

I was given a choice
A difficult choice

I could remain the 7 year old child
I was right now in this reality
and the life I had been living
would be immediately destroyed
and I would start over again
as myself at 7 years old

BUT... the life I had lived so far
would be a non entity and
all its happenings and memories
would be forever erase.

I would start over and have
no idea of the journey to come
or how it would unfold and end

I couldn't decide
But I was told I must decide
or name a proxy.

I looked at the beautiful, winged creature
that brought me to this place and time
Our eyes locked and our thoughts met

I nodded
and the creature's thoughts
told me it would make the decision for me
... and it did

I awake as usual to the me I know
unaware of the trip I had been on

I reach for my phone to see the time
and my screen is totally different

It displays a nondescript pale beige moth
on the right-hand side of the screen
and a beautiful technicolor winged creature
is displayed on the left-hand side

It all seems so strange
and yet so very familiar

I look out my window at the beach,
the ocean, the seagulls, the sand
and somehow they seem unreal

So, I walk down to the shore
and pick up a smooth thin stone,
snap my wrist and flick it
into the still of the water;
the stone skips 7 times

I take up a handful of sand
and let is slip through my fingers

I all seems so strange and unreal
    but it's not... it's real

    AND

    I'm alive!
     Again!

10 PAK -3 The Long Poems – *Candice James*

Time

10 PAK -3 The Long Poems – *Candice James*

The twilight of night flickers
      and flares
dancing with its own reflections

The hard-edged rectangle of time
chafes at the edges of the world

All is ghostly and surreal
but textured in its vapid mist

Dreams, memories, and the past
glow in the shade of a long-ago star

Pieces of days and bits of nights
share the same trajectory of time
 if there is such a thing as time

Dusk burns softly into charcoal ash
then rekindles into a fiery dawn

I step back
into a brand-new moment,
a long time lost,
and gaze into the eternity of days

In a ghostly glow of misty reflections
I see myself in a fading blue mirror
fade ... fading away

I am here I am there
I am everywhere
I am the static motionless passage
of hours, minutes and seconds

I am a moment in time

    a never-ending
    moment in time

And then,

Time shatters
The moment and I fade out
as if we never existed,
as if we never were.

Time ... is not.

Rain

10 PAK -3 The Long Poems – *Candice James*

The rain gathers
then spills on me
I am aware of it's texture
but unaffected by its wet

I am not of this world
I am of the stars

I am your desire
I am your thirst
I am the white light
deep inside the dark
I am your prisoner
You are my freedom

I was naked in my heart
and drunk in my soul
I had no pride   I was fallen.
You came and rescued me
but I can't recall your name
or visualize your face

You are yesterday's wind
a murmur on the breeze
an indecipherable love song

I have been visiting with angels
and they sang my night awake
and the wind whispered my name
and called me to its side
then I remembered your name
and could visualize your face

And you looked just like me

For a moment I was confused
then I heard an angel say
"This is one of the other *yous*"

Then the angel suggested
I think deeply and write
another untitled poem to myself
and to all my other selves

Later that night I heard the voice
of someone seeking my warmth.

All night I wrote technicolor songs
with double-clutched bass lines
and thunderous drum rolls
and softly brushed cymbals
to accent the feel of the rain
that kept falling all night long

And the rain keeps falling
falling so softly
I almost can't hear it

I am asleep
inside this indigenous dream
but still aware
on the quantum level

And I wonder...
who will stop the rain

Stone Night

10 PAK -3 The Long Poems – *Candice James*

The dark is closing in
on the freezing fist of frost

I am alone in this stone night
existing in this inexistence
of crashing nothingness
that has rendered me deaf

I strum the back of the wind
and sing a gilded lament
to the ebony ravens
that they may carry
past tense love letters
to the broken hearted

I am alone in this stone night

Dark clouds billow white
Rogue waves calm themselves

Melting snowflakes chill the air
so they may survive one more minute
in this passage of time
that never passes
and remains suspended
in a proportionless
insomniac static

Alive in the film of forever,
I rewind my memories:
To spin them real
To see your face
To feel your hand in mine
       again ...
if only for a moment

Outside the weather is changing

I hear the tick of rain
washing the dusty exterior
of my single-pane windows

Its rhythm is sporadic and unkempt
like day-old unfolded laundry
    reminding me
of things left undone

I never did say "I love you" enough
I wonder now if I ever did actually say it

    I should have
    and would have

    if I'd known then
    what I know now

We never know
the depth of the ocean
even when we dive deep
into its full effulgence

We never know
how much we love someone
until they are no long here

Hindsight is always 30/20

    Always

I never knew myself
in all the years I was

And even now I know
I don't really know myself
and probably never will

I remember
on a cold day in August
saying my silent goodbye
in heartfelt soliloquy
as you left this world

    and even now,
        still,
inside this stone cold night
      the old
  Winchester Cathedral
song lyrics come to mind —

Oh-bo-de-oh-doe
Oh-bo-de-oh-doe
Oh-bo-de-oh-doe
de doe-duh

Vision and Impressions of the 7th Kind

10 PAK -3 The Long Poems – *Candice James*

A creamy caramel flavored
cotton candy day
permeates the thin layer of air
floating in an invisible halo
      above
    my head
surrounding my thoughts

And I drift and dream ...
drift, drift, and dream
of yesterday's carnivals
and carousel rides

I imagine ice-cream mountains
melting in the salty mouth of the ocean.
and daylight stars crinkling
and winking in parodied unison
at the scene unfolding behind
the eyes of a fading fantasy
slowly becoming a reality

Then suddenly!
A calamity of echoes
rocks the foundation of sound

The weight of the wet
threatens to drown me
then sheds its tears
to mix with mine
        and
    in a heartbeat
the nightmare is slain

Then ...
the heartbeat falters
    and s t o p s ...
and a new dream begins to rise
above the ice-cream mountains
as daylight stars slowly wax
into the gathering twilight
and ushers in a silver scarf
    of opalescence
to adorn the neck of the ebony sky

The weight of the wet dissipates
    I grow wings to fly
    I become the air

I float for an eternity and then
I'm walking down a lane
of broken branches,
that whisper fading promises
to the gullible breeze

The wind howls and calls my name
and assaults the unsuspecting trees
in frail retaliation seeking payment
for the forsaken wounded dreams
harbored in the inky saps
of the stillborn sapling children

    Ground level
the leaves rustle and groan
as a small field mouse rushes headlong
into his own private green ecstasy.

There seems to be no reason or rhyme
no signposts or scheme
to this rustling and rushing ...

    but there is ...

On some other quatum level
a group of watchers are watching
and as their camera eyes zoom in
they start chanting and moving the leaves,
in a semi-circular moon shadow pattern
    on a flat sky filled with
    crescent-shaped moons
    triangular stars
    and the broken branches
    of the dead sapling children

The outlaw stars shed their scars
with wild and frivolous abandon
to the wind and haze of a bruised rain

They introduce the dream
    over and over
   again and again
   until it spins real

I am blessed with supine thoughts
slicing through the ether into my mind
that I may pierce this dying paper sermon
with the blade of my scriptured pen
and bring a brand-new world alive

A world of colors and letters
and pieces of heart and mind
all coalesced in the crux of a kiss;
a kiss to awaken the nerves
of a universe sleeping in my dreams
that I may loose them into a becoming
with new visions and impressions
as my eyes become refracting telescopes
with a million expanding apertures

After spending lifetimes on the 5th level
I have morphed into the 6th level
where visions and impressions of the 7th
kind are now seen in their entirety
      and refined clarity
      and finally ...
   finally I understand

10 PAK -3 The Long Poems – *Candice James*

Leaving And Staying

10 PAK -3 The Long Poems – *Candice James*

Further afield,
on a summer hillside,
a rainbow holds the echo
of a wet aftermath of sea salt
and tears and rain
borrowed from a lingering gypsy midnight
alive with moons and stars and comets
streaking old sundowns anew
in this dawn of lost recollections

This is a time of leaving and staying
This is a time of naked truths
A time of rising and falling
A time of living and dying

This is the breath of existence
and the exhalation of annihilation

As the day moves into static oblivion
only a few remnants
of the afternoon remain

Little glowing bits of dark and light

Fodder and blankets
for the impending night

As I loosened the ribbon in midnight's hair
the hidden stars came tumbling down
    in a faux waterfall
   of schemes and dreams

 I fell into a restless, fitful sleep
fraught with visions of hope and torment

High above the snowline, in rapturous glory,
stood a glistening, towering ice palace

I feared I would freeze to death
as I deigned to close in on it
but the closer I came
the warmer the air was

As the heat built to a summer high
     the ice refused to melt

     It stood tall
on its principled dias of integrity

Later as the evening fell in dark drapes
      a white dove soared
in the moonlit meadow

I could hear the din and crash of waves
but there were no oceans near or far

I tried to kick night's blankets off
      to envision the grasp
and clasp the approaching dream

Alas... no use
The parading of ghosts was a haze

Faces and bodies were fading figurines
blurring into a make-believe city
stumbling and crumbling into fine dust
for the hungry wind to feed on

I watched the struggle
   of dust and wind
      dancing
in a bizarre broken rhythm
for what seemed like an eternity

Then finally, appetite sated,
the wind moved into the arms of night
      and fell asleep
    perchance to dream
in this fragile and surreal motion
        of leaving
          and
         staying.

10 PAK -3 The Long Poems – *Candice James*

Frayed Edges

10 PAK -3 The Long Poems – *Candice James*

Stand
      on the pinnacle of a star
and meld its shine
      into your eyes

Let the stardust
flow through your fingers
like satin and silk
spun from heaven's loom

Gaze on the beauty of your essence
as your soul comes forth
    and undresses
In beauty, pomp and glory
In sorrows torn and bruised

In faith and hope
on a wing and a prayer
relying on a perilous handshake,
the spirit flies into the pastoral storm
braving the winds and rains
    and tidal bores
to enjoy its short hour in the sun
and then is seen no more …

    in that disguise

But it returns
again and again

In shades
of black and blue
In days of happiness
laced with tears
In nights of lust
flavored with spice.

the spirit becomes a grimace
slowly morphing into a smile

then a teardrop
burning inside an icicle

    and then
in a moment of eternal grace
   a waterfall springs
   from a desert dune

A snowflake falls
from a hot summer sky
A raindrop returns
to the ocean
and a rolling mist
blends and hides
inside a clear blue sky
of illusions

I move in and out of myself
changing skin and bones and hair
like frayed and worn-out clothes
inside the changing rooms of life

Alive among the dead and missing
dead in a world of the living
it's impossible to come to terms
with where I am at any given time

I am an atom and an electron
a proton and a neutron
a muon and a quark
moving inside a mercurial molecule

rocking and rolling
in the cylinder of eternity
in a scientific hall of religious chants

where sense and nonsense
square dance and spin
inside the waltz of the flowers
at rest in the Garden of Eden

Standing outside myself
propped up in the doorway of chance
    I am leaning
on the broken crutch of hope

Sitting resolute
in a gambler's faux paradise
I am clutching at the straw in my drink

Shifting foot to foot
at the racetrack
I am trying to keep my binoculars
steady and focused

When I lose I win
When I win I lose

Everything is an anachronism unto itself
and I am a poor player in a starring role
standing small, front and centre,
on a make-shift stage of fools

What most I am
that least I seem

There used to be cool days
and hot nights.
Colorful beach balls
and high flying kites
Rolling across a flashing neon sky

There used to be precious moments
adorned with pebbles becoming pearls
cloistered in the oyster dreams
I secreted in my questing soul

Looking back, my vision is 30/20
I see myself and my long ago loves

The yesteryear film rolls
snips and snaps by

A rogues' gallery
of good and bad choices
soft satin whispers
and harsh raspy voices

Sometimes I left a love affair
torn and bruised
Sometimes I left a lover
applauding my exit

And sometimes
I lingered a too long
and the air became
a scraping fingernail
on the blackboard
of my caged redemption

I imagine Blake and Coleridge
wrapped up in silk
mending the frayed edges
of my ragged spirit

Sometimes I imagine them
as master musicians
in jazz symphonies

If I listen closely
for their music
I can almost hear it

The frost on the grass
has disappeared
and the dew on the rose
has evaporated

But I am still here
moving in and out of myself
in a comedy of errors
and a self-made tragedy
of broken promises
and wasted wishes

When will I ever learn

I've come to realize
there is no such thing
as balance or imbalance

There is only distribution
viscosity, swagger and sway
and there is no such thing
as a pristine existence

There are no circles, squares,
rectangles or triangles,
only human fabrics
with fading patterns
with unraveling seams

We wear living garments
ripped, worn and torn

We are the frayed edges
of our own design

I Rise

10 PAK -3 The Long Poems – *Candice James*

Locked in a perpetual wave
of 'now' and 'then' and 'when',
I collide with drunken stars
on a shiny indigo highway
of technicolor wounds and scars

There comes a sudden speculation
leading to a startling revelation
of buried forgotten memories
clawing their way out of oblivion
into the halls of remembrance

In the deep recesses of the psyche
where the spirit and soul
      hold hands
and sometimes embrace
I gaze, with sorrow and smiles,
down the roads I didn't take.

Dust on the doorstep
and streaks on the windows,
the house I call home and live in
has seen laughter and tears
and a bevy of better days

Every journey is salt and pepper.
light and dark interspersed
on a blanket of hopes and dreams
abandoned in the pit of a mineshaft.
A mineshaft of our own making

I see yesterday's trinkets and toys:

a stuffed animal with one eye
a doll with a broken arm
a carriage with crooked wheels
a bicycle with no handlebars

And, somewhere, over the rainbow,
I rise dignified and exalted
in an invisible universe of sighs

Sighs that speak of my merits
and applaud my distinguished failures
before a crowd of my enemies

Friends have long left the area

And from within this angry arena,
still, I rise dignified and undamaged
   exalted and crowned
with glorious barbs and weeds

I rise again and again
as a broken-winged phoenix
charred and burned and ashen
in a wildfire of my own creation

I have become
an out-of-control candle
flickering
in the wind and rain,
dampened
by the tears of the sun
in a tropical forest
of flammable lakes

Ghostly echoes of the dead
are closing in on me fast

Soon I will be fully ensconced
in their pale gray realm of mist

I hear the beating of a distant drum
and the whispers of an angel singing,
calling my name, calling me home
      after I've surrendered
      and lost, this,
  my private hundred years war

I feel my heartbeat slowing
my eyelids closing
my breath dissipating

Everything is moving in slow motion
       then it stops

    then I stop

This is the last page
of the book I am

I rise no more

I am dead

AUTHOR PROFILE

Candice James is a professional poet, musician, singer, songwriter and visual artist. She was appointed Poet Laureate Emerita of New Westminster BC by order if City Council in November 2016 after serving 2 back to back three-year terms as Poet Laureate. She is founder of Royal City Literary Arts Society, and Fred Cogswell Award For Excellence in Poetry and past president of the Federation of BC Writers. She's a full member of the League of Canadian Poets and the author of 28 books of poetry through 6 Publishing Houses.

Her first book A SPLIT IN THE WATER was published in 1979 by Fiddlehead Poetry Books, University of New Brunswick CANADA Her awards include Pandora's Collective Citizen of the Year; Bernie Legge Platinum Awards Artist of the Year.

www.ingramcontent.com/pod-product-compliance
Lightning Source LLC
Chambersburg PA
CBHW071242070526
44583CB00017B/2294